MW00849099

Theses Towards
a Trinitarian Ontology

THESES TOWARDS A TRINITARIAN ONTOLOGY

⊕

Klaus Hemmerle

Foreword by
Dr. Rowan Williams

Translated by
Stephen Churchyard

❧ Angelico Press

First published as *Thesen zu einer
trinitarischen Ontologie* by Johannes in 1976
First published by Angelico Press, 2020
© Angelico Press 2020

Our thanks to the Diocese of Aachen for their
kind permission to publish this English translation

For information, address:
Angelico Press
169 Monitor St.
Brooklyn, NY 11222
angelicopress.com

978-1-62138-649-0 pb
978-1-62138-650-6 cloth

Cover Design: Michael Schrauzer

CONTENTS

Foreword

Dr. Rowan Williams

It is easy to misunderstand a question like "What is it that really *is*?" In the history of modern (and not only modern) philosophy, we have got used to a kind of stand-off between a number of problematic positions relating to the question. Perhaps we need to go back to what is imagined to be a pre-modern innocence about this and claim that human thought simply has access to what's "out there." Perhaps we should develop some version of the idea that something is "out there" which remotely conditions what we can say or think, but that any granular connection with what we actually say or think is completely inscrutable to us. Perhaps we are tempted to settle for the oddly self-undermining conclusion that "thinking" is itself an illusion, a physically determined set of sensations which can make no claim to represent anything.

All these approaches share one fundamental assumption, which is that the problem in question is about how we connect an otherwise unconnected pair of realities, an "inside" and an "outside." The legacy of German idealism is a mixed and controverted one, but at least it has left a saving trace of dissatisfaction with this polarity. What if, after all, our thinking about thinking (about the entire business of responding consistently to an environment) were indeed the only place to start coping with the question of what actually "is"? Because the crucial fact about thinking is that it is not an activity we choose to undertake; we are implicated in it as soon as we are bodily realities—which is to say, from the first moment of our existence as a coherent organic system. Before we know it we are connecting, representing, strategizing, positing—"speaking" to ourselves before we have a full verbal resource to work with. To put it another way, our human existence as coherent organisms is inseparable from the pattern of intelligent reaction to what is not ourselves. Our identity is always already shaped by *response*: we have a place within a flow of agency that does not originate in a fixed and context-free interiority. "Thinking is found always already or first of all in the process itself," as Bishop Hemmerle puts it in #20 of this remarkable essay—in the process of agency or energy unceasingly moving "out" from self-identity into relation, or rather, much more accurately, exhibiting and realizing identity in a relatedness that is never absent. What *is* is in motion, and not only in motion but in a motion that includes otherness in its own action and definition.

We can represent this with a touch of the mythical by seeing it as a ceaseless process of the "renunciation" of prior self-identity, a ceaseless reception into identity of what it is not, so that this "what it is not" is as it were generated by identity for identity to be itself. The basic structure of the world that is revealed *in* (not simply *by*) thinking is not an ensemble of atomistic substances but a flow of interaction in which every identifiable "node" or "pole" (Hemmerle's preferred term) of active existence receives and gives substantive uniqueness to every other so that no thing stands alone. As Hemmerle puts it in a powerful and provocative image, our best way of understanding the process of the world—and so, of speech and thought—is perhaps to see it as *play* (#22). What I am in the course of a game—or, for that matter, in the performing of an artwork—is entirely bound up with what is *given* me to receive and answer. What is given me to receive and answer is already what is made possible and real as a receiving and answering; and so on, in a reciprocity without beginning. If that is so, not only the polarity between inside and outside but that between active and passive, or between totality and individuality or between sameness and difference all demand to be looked at afresh.

What Hemmerle argues, with exceptional clarity and conceptual ambition, is that only the vocabulary of Trinitarian theology can provide a home for this understanding of our speech and thought. It is certainly not that we somehow speculate that God "must" be a plurality of personal agency because the world is as it is. But the narrative of God's redeeming love, the specific historical shape of how we speak of God's act to renew creation and heal our fallen state, unfolds in such a way that it dictates a certain grammar in our talk about God. It is shaped as a picture of self-giving, abandonment to the other, "displacement of the center of gravity from the self to the other" (#18), divine "selfhood" or identity being realized in an irreducible pattern of interaction, and so on; and this pattern can be recognized as completing and contextualizing the pattern loosely discerned in the logic of finite being and human speech.

And if this is so, we can say that "revealed religion" is indeed the revealing not of an unexpected extra item in the universe but of *the character of active existence itself*: the trinitarian doctrine and the incarnational narrative that triggers its formulation declare what it is to *be*. There is nothing more fundamental to be said than the affirmation that the pure act, the unconstrained and unlimited initiative on which all finite reality depends, is itself relational. And because the effect of its action within our history is the relation we can only designate as love, we understand the eternal pattern of identity in otherness as a love that overflows in and for what it is not, for the finite world that arises, freely but not arbitrarily, out of the nature of God as gift and as giver.

"I can only see whatever I permit to be given to me; I can only see that to which I give myself" (#32). Just as thinking itself can be thought only within the actuality of engagement with an agency that is not itself, so theology in particular can take place only within the always-already of gift and love. And Hemmerle's brief but pregnant concluding paragraphs firmly locate not only theology but the entire life of the Christian community within the flow and process of divine self-giving. Theology "depends upon living with each other and seeing each other" (#33). But this in turn implies that the Church itself is not an alien collectivity with hostile designs upon individual liberty, nor yet an association of like-minded human egos, but "*life itself.*" Its ethical and spiritual disciplines are not markers of identity for a specific human grouping but the expressions of the ontological truth which it embodies. Hemmerle's language here, deliberately or not, echoes the way in which Eastern Christian theologians, from Khomyakov in nineteenth-century Russia to Yannaras in twentieth-century Greece, have insisted that ethics and spirituality must be seen first and foremost as a matter of the character of ecclesial life, not of imposed rules; ethical integrity is to do with life and death rather than right and wrong. And the model of how tradition works in theology likewise echoes themes from the Eastern Christian world in stressing how theology must live in an openness to the full ongoing life of self-giving love and prayer in the Church across the ages. Not the least of the gifts which these pages offer is a vision of a genuinely traditional and ecumenical theology, recognizable across confessional boundaries.

These theses were written originally in tribute to Hans Urs von Balthasar, and their debt to so many themes in Balthasar's writing is manifest; the ecumenical vision just mentioned is certainly a Balthasarian perspective. But—despite the rapidly burgeoning literature on Balthasar—this text has for too long been allowed to sit on the shelves or in the margins of theological discussion. As a new generation of theologians returns with fresh perspective and fresh energy to questions around the metaphysical implications of doctrinal confession and interacts more robustly with the philosophical aporias of our time, Bishop Hemmerle's closely argued but always lucid arguments are coming into their own. It is a real blessing to have them set out here for English-speaking students and lovers of theology; and we can hope and pray for a lively, critical, and grateful response in the doctrinal and philosophical reflections of the years ahead.

Author's Preface

In August last year, for Hans Urs von Balthasar's seventieth birthday, I wrote him an extended birthday card, "Theses towards a Trinitarian ontology." In Balthasar's work, I find an alternative to a theology with a merely anthropological approach, which attributes human needs and human modes of understanding to God, but also an alternative to a static and deductive theological thinking, which degrades the events of salvation by making them into examples of a metaphysics conceived of as valid in itself. In Balthasar's thought, nothing of the plenitude of dogma, nothing of the way in which that plenitude is developed by the thinkers of the tradition, is deleted, or deflected by hermeneutic sleight of hand—yet, at the same time, the historical and event-like character which we find in the immediacy of Scripture is in no way minimized. The speculative daring, the discriminating precision, to which patristic and scholastic theology attained, are not relegated to the museum. The dynamics of historical thinking, the transformation in our perspectives for understanding Being which have been fashioned by contemporary consciousness, do not remain outside the doors of the church. This, of course, first of all, and most profoundly, concerns theology itself. But it is clear enough that Balthasar's work addresses, and, indeed, transforms structures of thinking, modes of seeing, the encounter with reality, and the ways in which persons act. Not only theology, but philosophy and spirituality, are made new; and this not from just any direction, but from out of the heart of our faith, from the Christ-event read in a Trinitarian way.

Does not the stimulus given in this way by a Hans Urs von Balthasar impel us towards a new, a Trinitarian ontology? I understood my "birthday card" as the formulation of this question, as both an answer to, and as a way of thanking, Balthasar. In the present version I have made some additions and clarifications, but have retained the character of the original—fragmentary and incompletely demonstrated in its argumentation and conclusions as it was. I should like, in this way, to pose to the reader of this little volume that question to which Balthasar's thought has compelled me.

Aachen, January 1976
Klaus Hemmerle

I

New Ontology as a Theological and Philosophical Postulate

1. The Question of a New Ontology

Ontology, the theory of beings and Being, has been conspicuously pushed aside from the center of scholarly interest. Ontology can only be of interest where the questions, "what is Being in itself? what are beings in themselves?" are regarded as meaningful ones. These ways of posing the question are already overlaid and displaced by several developmental thrusts. The possibility of ascertaining facts, and the explanation of those facts by means of binding laws of nature or demonstrable historical contexts, stood at the center of "classical" science and scholarship. Such a "classical" scholarship, still widely influential on popular consciousness, is more and more eroded by a functional manner of thinking and observing. Neo- and post-positivistic thinking, neo- and post-Marxist thinking, are not so much concerned with facts in themselves as with their effects, with their relation to needs and the practical consequences. For such positions, to ask what Being or beings might be in themselves is to ask too little, since the question asks about something which, supposedly, does not reach as far as life or as far as praxis. On the other

9

hand, it also asks too much, since it asks about something which cannot possibly be verified, explained, or made use of. Ontology becomes superfluous, *l'art pour l'art*.

This, in its turn, also affects theology. Has not the New Testament already, through the dogmas and the theology of the church councils, been infiltrated by Greek metaphysics? Has not ontology thereby become a danger to theology? This is the sort of thing one hears from all quarters. Systematically and historically, efforts are made to go back to the pre-metaphysical and pre-ontological level of the origins. The metaphysically drafted declarations of Christology and of the doctrine of the Trinity apparently say too much. They do not seem to have been arrived at through historical data; they do not seem to be translatable into anything which is intelligible to us today. They also, apparently, say too little: their "objectivity" does not answer to the needs and questions of human beings. Everyone wants to get back behind ontology. And at the same time everyone also wants to get beyond ontology. Theology ought to become practical, functional, anthropological.

And yet my thesis is as follows: We need an ontology. This postulate is meant both theologically and philosophically.

We need an ontology for theology's sake.

This becomes clear when we examine the positions taken up by any theology which renounces ontology.

The first amongst these would be a theology which would establish Christian facts and themes and which would bring them into relation with facts and themes from the history of religion, and from intellectual history, by explaining, comparing, and distinguishing the two. If this were all, then theology, and even revelation itself, would no longer be distinguishable from the history of religion or from intellectual history. For how would we be able to articulate what is unique in and proper to revelation, that which revelation is *of itself*? Mere history at best relates what is Christian to a framework which remains external to it.

There are other possibilities. Theology might restrict itself to declaring what revelation uniquely is only in respect to the needs and requirements of human beings—to understanding revelation only from the standpoint of the questions brought to it by human beings. Ontology would, here, simply be equated with anthropology; the question of what God or His Word are, or say, in themselves would again fall away. In such an approach, however, the Christian answer would run the risk of being only a result of the human question.

Looked at from yet another angle, theology might drop the whole question of what God of Himself is, says, or gives. It could concern itself only with the human answer, and become a guide to ethical action. But would not God's gift, the gift of God, who gives Himself, dissolve, in this way, into a mere demand for that gift?

Finally, theology might arrive at the idea—and it has already arrived at it—of positing God's otherness and transcendence in so absolute a fashion that all assertions, all self-assertion could only be a reproach [*Verweis*], and could never in any way, any longer, be a testimony [*Vorweis*]. Faith would dwindle to a declaration of faith, *fides quae* [faith in something] would founder into *fides qua* [faith as something]. The impulse unconditionally to let God be God would be changed into its direct opposite: God would become a mere vanishing point, essentially powerless over human beings and the world. His transcendence would no longer have sufficient force to reach our immanence.

Theologically, therefore, it is precisely ontology—the visibility and expressibility of the meaning of Being— which permits the unfolding of that which God, from His own primordiality, wishes to say, to give, and to be.

But we also need ontology for philosophy's sake. If philosophy believes that it must restrict itself to theory of science, to logic, or to pragmatic plans for personal or social action, then it has a duty to set out its reasons for this belief. These reasons, however, unavoidably extend into the ontological domain. Even someone who says that the question of the meaning of Being is meaningless has already decided in advance upon the meaning of Being. Only reflection on the main pre-decisions, however, can meet the demands of a critical reason. Only a philosophy which acknowledges and argues for its own understanding of Being can count as self-reflective.

An ontology which has to be posited together with theology, so that theology can remain theology, and which has to be laid bare in philosophy, so that philosophy can remain philosophy, is, admittedly, more than a philosophical treatise. It asks, instead, about the meaning of Being, about that fundamental decision which does not only concern human beings, but which concerns the fact that anything at all exists and not nothing; it asks about that light in which all our seeing and saying takes place. The ontology which is overdue today is a radical, a fundamental ontology.

2. The Field of the Answer: the Reciprocal Relationship between Theology and Ontology

Theology and philosophy, therefore, have equally acute difficulties with ontology today.

In the course of its history, theology has often, indeed, essentially, always, fallen back upon ontological pre-decisions and pre-understandings furnished by the thinking which is contemporary with it or which is handed down by tradition. Greek philosophy is not only the medium in which the fundamental dogmas were expressed; the whole way in which the patristic literature thinks and expresses itself betrays many signs of Platonic, Aristotelian, and Stoical undercurrents. The way in which a new reception of Aristotelianism shaped high scholasticism has been decisive for theology up until the present day, however much nominalism, rationalism, and post-idealism left their marks on the "scholasticism" of the sixteenth to the nineteenth centuries.

Admittedly, theology has often, by introducing what is proper to it, furnished and further developed ways of posing ontological questions and ontological conceptu-

13

alities, brought out by the measure which theology brings with it. The answers given at Nicaea and Chalcedon, for instance, are, precisely, not merely applications of Greek philosophy, but transformations of it.

In the reciprocal relationship between theology and philosophy, there lies, perhaps, even today, a chance for the reconquest of ontology; this would be significant both for theology and for philosophy.

3. Introduction: God's Word in Human Words

First, let us start with an assertion which, once again, is philosophical *and* theological. If God reveals Himself to human beings, if God speaks a divine word to humanity, then this happens in human words.

This assertion is *philosophical*; it proposes conditions for human thinking, amongst which is found the hypothesis of a self-revealing God, a hypothesis which cannot be accessed, constructed, or demonstrated by philosophy. The fact that God cannot speak to human beings in any other way than in words which human beings understand, which, therefore, must be human words, is to be gathered from human thinking. And human thinking knows that God—if He reveal Himself—cannot leap over this necessity for human thinking. There are, therefore, transcendental conditions which are clear to thinking and which are an anticipation of thinking about that which (or He who) is *per definitionem* higher than, and removed from, thinking and its conditions.

Philosophy has drawn various consequences from this state of affairs.

Either it concludes that human thinking is superordinate even to a revelation of God, and to a God who reveals Himself; if it does not reflect any further on this superordination, but takes it as final, then in the last analysis it arrives at a rejection of any God who can reveal Himself.

Or, conversely, philosophy asks itself what its own transcendental claim might mean. It reflects on the fact that the priority given to thinking before a self-revealing God, and the priority of a self-revealing God before thinking, are of different kinds, that a philosophical *a priori* for theology and a theological *a priori* for philosophy have different meanings. Only in such reflection, however, does thinking become truly "transcendental," that is to say, become so extensive that it has space even for what transcends thinking, yet which, as such, also enters thinking.

The assertion that God, if He speak His word, must speak it in human language, is a *theological* one. For that God should surrender what is proper to Him to an interpretative horizon which is determined by what is proper to another, by another's possibilities—by what is proper to and possible to human beings, precisely—that God, who comes before everything, should come, in His word, after another, is an assertion of singular import about God.

4. The Fortunes of God's Word in the Human Word; The Fortunes of the Human Word in God's Word

Let us remain with the *theological* reflection, the proposition that God to such an extent speaks His divine word into a human word, that His own word, the divine word, is attainable only through the human word. In this word it is no longer possible to separate the human and divine components from each other; for how could we grasp what is divine in this word in any other way than, in turn, through human words?

The relation between God's word and the human word in the word of revelation is, however, a manifold one. The word sent by God shelters itself beneath the presuppositions of a supposedly human word. If God's word were not attached to an already existing human word, then it would say nothing to human beings. Here, however, the human word is retrospectively claimed by the word to which it in the first place owes its own existence; the human word which precedes God's word is, ontologically, subsequent to the word which makes the human being possible as a being with language, and which, thereby, makes language itself possible. The human word to which revelation lays claim is, therefore, brought back home to itself, to its origin, and is raised above itself.

At the same time, God's word also "rises" above itself, in that it condescends to becomes a word in a human word, a word among human words. God's word is of itself the power to let an Other be. In that this word becomes one of the conditions of possibility of its Other, however, in that it relinquishes itself into the human word, it takes on the shape of powerlessness: it becomes susceptible to misunderstanding and misuse. Yet in this powerlessness it also gains something: it becomes actual in the medium of its Other; it becomes, indeed, the actuality of its Other. It is precisely in this process, which means both relinquishment and elevation, that revelation takes place.

This characteristic of the relationship is not an addition to the content of revelation; it already *is* its content. God is identity with Himself in going beyond Himself, in giving Himself away. To this extent what happens to the word of God in revelation is just the same as what happens, conversely, to the human word: self-lowering, self-relinquishment, self-surpassing.

5. The Double *A Priori* of Theology

Each word of revelation and each theology undergo a double, counter-turning movement. God's word becomes one of the conditions of human understanding. Human self-understanding is therefore a pre-supposition, an allowance, and a pre-judice [*Voraussetzung, Vorgabe, und Vor-urteil*] given in order that God's word may be brought to givenness. Yet at the same time human speaking and understanding has to give itself up to that of which it is not on its own account capable, to that which is its own presupposition and fulfilment; it has to take its measure from that which enters into human speaking and understanding, but which enters as what surpasses them.

In revelation and in theology, therefore, a double *a priori* holds sway: the *a priori* of the divine for the human and the *a priori* of the human for the divine.

But this last *a priori* is divine too, an *a priori* "from above," for it has the ground of its possibility in the condescension, in the unfathomable freedom of the God who reveals Himself and who gives Himself away. Just this freedom is testified to in the necessity of an approach to revelation and to theology which is *also* anthropological; a *purely* anthropological approach to revelation and to theology is thereby superseded.

6. Two Fundamental Types: Theology of Translation and Theology of Witness

Historically, various types of theology have been developed, and there are, here, two legitimate basic positions.

In the first, what is proper to the word of revelation, what is other in it, is formulated from the standpoint of a human, historical, philosophically pre-formed mode of questioning and of understanding, and is related to and retrieved by that human approach. One might call this a "translating theology." Perhaps the greatest example is Aquinas's "Aristotelianism."

In the other basic position, human thinking relies on God's radical beginning, His revelation, and acquires anew, from this approach, the possibilities of human thinking and speaking: a witnessing [*bezeugende*] theology, a generative [*zeugende*] theology. Here, despite his "Platonism" and "Augustinianism," might belong, for example, Bonaventure.

In neither type is there a question of the reduction of theology to only one of its two *a prioris*, but of a difference in the center of gravity, a difference in the approach on the basis of which, in each case, the double *a priori* comes into play.

7. The Historical Contribution of Theology to Ontology

The double *a priori* of theology played a powerful role precisely in the formation of the fundamental dogmas and theologoumena in Christology and in the doctrine of the Trinity.

In respect of the development of dogmatic theology in the first centuries of Christianity, there has been, not without reason, talk of a Hellenization of Christian thinking, of the entry of biblical kerygma under the sign of a metaphysics pre-formed by Greek thought. The difference between the thought and speech of the Bible, and the thought and speech of the late-antique theological tradition, is often pointed out. If in fact Christianity had happened historically to have developed against a different background of thinking, culture, and language, the form of its transmission and its theology would certainly have looked different.

Nevertheless, we must also, at the same time, consider the contrary movement; indeed, that contrary movement must be still more strongly emphasized. Faith's very resistance to being merely subsumed under Greek and Hellenistic metaphysical categories of thinking released new possibilities of expression and comprehension. We can think, here, of the overcoming of Arianism, which grew out of a Middle Platonism; or we can think of the strenuous elaboration of the fundamental concepts of Christology and of the doctrine of the Trinity, concepts which were not readily available from philosophy. The concrete contingencies of the history of dogma and theology, the extra-theological and extra-philosophical considerations and conditions impinging on them, do not cancel out the rigorousness of the development of theology, nor the rigor of its outcome. The adoption of ready-made conceptual categories leads to further critical and creative development.

8. The Historical Deficit of a Christian Ontology

Without at this point going into detail about that which is proper to Christianity, and its dialogue with the conceptual models of the philosophical tradition, it is possible to summarize as follows. Christianity drove on the development of philosophy in a way both corrective and inspirational, both within and beyond theology, and allowed philosophy to acquire an ever more adequate form. Neither the great theologians nor the great theological schools betrayed what was distinctively Christian, nor did they sell it into slavery to a fundamentally alien ontology. We cannot orchestrate Heidegger's talk of a forgetting of Being in the history in philosophy with talk about a forgetting of faith in the history of theology.

Nevertheless, the other side of this point must also be dealt with: the distinctively Christian element did not comprehend the meaning of Being in advance; it did not lastingly reshape the approach of ontology as a whole. At any rate, the great attempts to find a genuinely Christian approach did not constitute the main current in the "schools" or in wider consciousness, and were not decisive in the subsequent history of thought.

In the symbiosis between Christianity and ontology, the Christian element continued to enjoy, almost unnoticed, the status of a guest amongst multiple philosophical projects and systems, the sources of whose formation lay elsewhere.

9. The Altered Situation at the End of Modernity

In the tradition of the West, taken as a whole, there was never really a uniform philosophy. The various competing approaches, schools, and models competed, however, on what was largely the same terrain. Today, at the end of the modern age, it is a pressing question whether there is any longer such a single terrain or common ground of philosophical thought, upon which this competition, and, therefore, mutual understanding, would be possible. At any rate, while it has become clearer which hitherto central currents of modern thought have become fragile, it has not yet been shown where a new foundation might be found, let alone a shared foundation.

A retrospective glance over the last few centuries, however, makes one thing clear. The specifically Christian element, which has so long and so enduringly been a determining force in the history of the West, has withdrawn ever further from general philosophical consciousness, from what has become of the philosophical tradition of antiquity and the Middle Ages in the course of the modern age.

How, though, is this Christian element to proceed? How can theology fulfil the postulate of its double *a priori*? For theology to return to a pre-modern age, to form shifting alliances with late modern and post-modern models of thought, or to renounce philosophy altogether, are impossible, or, at least, unsatisfactory, options. Might a new approach be pointed to by analyzing, on the one hand, just what it is that has come to an end with the end of the modern age, and, on the other, by reflecting on what it is that is proper to Christianity, and which has not, hitherto, taken a leading or epoch-making role in thinking? This, at least, is what the notion of a Trinitarian ontology aims at.

II

Entry Into
the Distinctively Christian
Element

10. Entering Into What is Distinctively
Christian

A new ontology is sought, an ontology which starts out from what is proper to Christianity. But whence does the properly Christian come into view? It cannot, in the present context, be specified by a historical investigation which reflects on singularities, parallels, and influences, nor by a systematic elaboration of what makes up the central content of the Christian faith. Instead a differential analysis is appropriate to what we have in mind here. In what way are the fundamental human experiences and fundamental understandings of God, the world, and human beings altered when faith in Jesus Christ breaks in upon them?

The double *a priori* under which theology stands can be seen in the following way: the attempt at the new, at the immediately Christian, is deciphered in the medium of the human, is read off from the "old," in which the newness of what is Christian is demonstrated.

11. Context: Religion

The experience of believing in Jesus Christ plays out, first of all, in the context of the fundamental human phenomenon of religion. Religion—and this goes for the Christian religion too—is distinguished from other inquiries into meaning and other final answers by a displacement, peculiar to religion, of its center of gravity. The human being no longer lives his life or understands his world from his own point of view, but rather from that of an Other who has withdrawn from him. The axis upon which life turns is not that of human questioning or human capacities, but that of the advent of this Other, of His irruption, His call, His epiphany, His communication, His revelation. This Other's overcoming of us is not, however, merely external: it discloses this Other as that upon which I and my world are most intimately dependent, and that from which I have most inwardly come to be.

The claim of religion is essentially *total*—and it is, in a twofold way, essentially *paradoxical*.

It is a paradox that I am not the center, not the starting point, that I do not live of my own accord, but that I cede the leading role, the whence and whither of my existence. It is equally a paradox that that which is other than everything and different from everything nevertheless becomes a part of everything, becomes something within everything's horizon, becomes something concrete amongst what is concrete. Religion is grounded in the transcendent's making an incursion into immanence without giving up its claim to be transcendent. One could speak of a reciprocal transcensus [*Transzenzus*].

In this way, religion finds itself in a twofold aporia, which leaves it, ever and again, questionable for human beings. On the one hand, religion's claim to be everything, to be the whole, is resisted by the I's ineliminable driving force, its interest, the necessity of initiating matters under which the I finds itself, the necessity of proceeding from out of itself. Religion becomes an exorbitant demand. On the other hand, the banality of everyday experience asserts itself; the urgency of the world and its relations vindicates itself against the claim of one particular relation to be the absolute relation. The claim of religion to be the most fundamental and most real relation appears as though it has been refuted by practicalities; this directly prompts the suspicion that religion is the unreal, is projection, is a mere addition to reality.

Human beings cannot, by themselves, completely solve this contradiction. They are either pressed down to the ground, squeezed into their own nothingness, by the weight of religion's claim, with "woe is me," in the end, as their last word; or they flee into the one and all of the divine. But in this latter way religion silently becomes a total and monistic system; the human being's encounter with the divine is annulled, and, essentially, both human and divine forfeit their station. Or, finally, human beings make religion "bearable" by reducing it, by means of compromise, re-interpretation, or clarification.

The only alternative from inside would be not to want to resolve this contradiction, but to endure ever new onsets of it, with an eye to hope.

12. Context: Experience of Logos

The experience of faith in Jesus Christ also plays out in another context, from which it is at the same time distinct: this can be described, to bring distinct phenomena very summarily together once again, as the experience of logos.

The human being starts out from himself. He discovers that he is present in everything which he discovers; he finds the traces of his own questioning and thinking in everything which his questioning and thinking encounter. The very connection, the way in which everything mirrors everything else, becomes a source of wonder, which fascinates him. His life means reconstructing this marvel, means wonderingly recovering the connection which he has discovered. He does not stand, as it were, over against religion, but right inside it. The last and the whole is greater than everything, and yet is in everything; but it is in everything not in a particular place, or in a particular way, but in everything as a whole, as the depth of everything.

Within this basic position—the experience of which has its place, as a moment, in Christianity too—there are various further positions. The 'I' is reduced to a mere moment of the self-perficient reason of totality and of the world; the world and totality are reduced to a mere moment of reason's path to itself, that reason which I am—either as this individual 'I', or as the subject, 'I' in a transcendental sense. Another position is the following: reflection dissolves the connection which links me with everything else into something questionable, or, even, something meaningless, which leaves only one option: resignation, despair, nihilism. Or again: reflection relinquishes its constructive power or its destructive impotence, and becomes contemplation, which sees and respects the connection, which takes it as read, without ever taking it upon itself to say by whom what is read was written—a pure philosophical *epochē*.

Such an experience of logos seems to make possible a limitless openness, even to be a transcendental openness, which can display and reveal whatever is. But is the All which can be experienced transcendentally really all there is? Wherever experience and the constructive capacity of the logos, wherever non-experience of the logos or experience of the non-logos, or wherever a merely transcendental openness posit themselves as absolute, wherever these claim absolute finality, there the breadth of logos-experience is reversed into a fundamental narrowing. When we stipulate that the logos should concern me only in and with respect to the whole, and not with respect to what concretely confronts me, are we not setting limits in advance to what is promised in the all-embracing logos?

13. Pre-liminary Answer: The Ancient Covenant

Religion and the experience of logos are contexts and contrasts for faith's encounter with Jesus Christ. The previous course of what belongs to and is proper to this faith takes place in Israel, in the religion of Yahweh.

In the religion of Yahweh, religion is made good and surpassed, and the fulfilment and overcoming of religion begins. Human beings stand over against God—but not only over against Him. Human beings are no longer left alone; God, too, stands on the side of human beings. For God is the God of the covenant; He is the God of the whole covenant, and therefore also supports and underwrites the other party to the covenant. The "woe is me" remains powerful, but God's hospitality, encouragement, and promise are more powerful.

The other aporia of religion is also unlocked, at least at first. However much Yahweh is the transcendent, the Other, He who is always greater, He is nevertheless just as much the God of history; life itself becomes the space of His revelation and the space in which He is encountered. The relationship to God includes the relationship to my neighbor. For the covenant is no longer one aspect of life alongside or beyond others, but embraces and governs all life's aspects and domains.

Even the experience of logos, however, is assimilated and surpassed; Yahweh is sole and transcendent, but He is not in competition with wisdom, which is mirrored in and which comes to fulfilment in all things, or with the logos, which reveals all connections and all secrets. Wisdom dwells with God, and the word, in which everything is created, lies with Him. He is the God of the All, revealed in everything, and is at the same time above it and over against it; He has the power to act and to speak concretely, and His word has the right to say something more and something new, beyond that which we can gather from the world by means of our thinking or our wonder.

14. The New Covenant's Answer to Religion and the Experience of logos

Christianity is a radicalization and a conversion of religion.

To live for the sake of God alone: this is the bearing of the conversion which corresponds to the coming of the Kingdom of God. Time is brought to fulfilment; the rhythm of mere hope culminates in a new, irrevocable present and presence of God. Human beings are called upon radically to forget their own age and to exchange it for the new age, that of the God who comes and who acts in Jesus Christ. One of the paradoxes of religion, to live for the sake of the Other, arrives, in this way, at its highest intensity.

The same thing also happens in the case of the second paradox. God enters, now that His dominion is dawning, into the horizon of history, and He does this in a singular, concrete place. There is no multiplicity of epiphanies; there is no longer any garland of revelations of the one secret; rather, the secret of the withdrawn God gathers and concentrates itself at a single point in history. This is the claim of Jesus, this the "stumbling-block" of His message.

Yet it is in this very intensification that religion experiences its conversion. The withdrawn source of everything, the God of the absolute origin and future, irrupts into a with-us and alongside-us. Our history, in a new sense, becomes His epiphany. It is no longer only as in the old covenant, in which God Himself repeatedly steers and changes history, and, so to speak, reaches out His hand from above to direct and to support us. No, God is now there Himself, in the same place where we are to give our answer. The fate of Jesus is God's solidarity with us and His proximity to us, in the middle of the space of our own experience, precisely at the site of our own impotence.

Religion, and even the experience of the logos, are thereby integrated, turned inside out, and surpassed. Everything which is enters an all-embracing context. But it is not exhausted by what my thinking can gather from the phenomena by means of analysis, design, critique, or contemplation. The word which the world speaks to me is no longer only its word or my word. Instead, history becomes the word spoken by the God who is revealed in it, who, appearing and acting at a single point, unconceals and confers the meaning of the whole. Its context becomes the context of my and of our existence, becomes a word which I and we consummate from our own origin—but as an answer, not as the enforcement of a law upon us or in us, but as a lived *up-towards*, from personal origin to personal origin.

15. The Inner Center of What is Christian: The Threefold Event

God's dominion is a conversion, a fulfilment and a surpassing of religion, and an experience of the logos—this, certainly, directs us towards the center of Christianity, but does not yet bring that center to light with the last clarity. We are directed towards this center by the Father's proposition: *Ipse est regnum caelorum.* He means Jesus Christ.

In that Jesus Christ announces and brings the dominion of God, and in that we encounter this dominion in Him, a radical, unreserved communication takes place between God and us. He Himself shares in Jesus all of what is ours and all of what is His. Nothing of His is left outside the gift which He gives us in Jesus Christ; nothing of ours is left outside history, which is God's own history.

Jesus Christ is, therefore, not merely an instrument of God's dominion, a dominion which would in some way remain above Him; and just as little is He God's demise, His losing of Himself into immanence, into the world and history. In Jesus, God comes into history in His entirety—and yet remains above it. Only where He remains over it is His presence in it curative and saving [*heil-sam*], redeeming.

The position of religion has changed: not a God above us, who presses us down into our own nothing or who sucks us up into His own all, but, instead, a God above us who encounters and answers the God who is among us, who catches, supports, and accepts us: we, between God and God.

Yet it is in just this way that we are ourselves. God does not merely do something *to* us when He gives us His Son, lets Him take on our flesh, lets Him, submissive even unto death, answer in our place. He does something *for* us, so that we, in Him, are able to do "the same thing" in Him and by virtue of Him. What unites the God above us and the God in us, unconditional love, the Holy Spirit, is given to us so that, by virtue of that Spirit, we ourselves, borne up by the Son, may give His upbearing answer.

Here for the first time, too, the solitary situation of the logos in the context of totality is unlocked into the single entire relationship which binds together irreducible opposition and unbreakable unity.

Trinity is not a logical abstraction from exaggerated individual scriptural statements; it is not speculation which busily stretches out tentative beginnings into cut-and-dried rationality. It is a statement of the fundamental experience of how human beings are newly given to God and newly given to themselves when they believe in Jesus Christ.

16. Consequence: Trinitarian Ontology

Our fundamental human situation, our thinking and being, indeed all Being, experiences a radical turning [*Umkehrung*] if God is the threefold, and, as the threefold, has His history in our history. This turning supersedes the measure of all thinking "contributed" by human beings about themselves, about God, about the world, about Being. A mere *relecture* of the ontological pre-understandings which accompany faith does not capture what is here disclosed and communicated to human understanding and being. The demand for a "new ontology," for a "Trinitarian ontology," is a consequence of this faith itself.

17. Approaches of the Tradition

Here we will recall the great thoughts about the Trinity offered by the Church Fathers, especially, and by Bonaventure. The latter incorporated—as Augustine in important respects also incorporated—a phenomenology of love into his speculations about Being, and revealed love as the ontological core not only of the mysteries of Christianity, but also of the Being of beings. The fundamental dogmatic definitions of the perichoresis of the Trinity and of the divine person as a *relatio subsistens* also point to the same context. Finally, here too belongs a thought which places *actus* (as in Aquinas) or *proportio* (as in Bonaventure and, for example, in Nicholas of Cusa) at the center.

These are all attempts in the direction indicated, but attempts which, historically, did not become decisive in the way which was aimed at. Any understanding of Being in which the latter is taken for self-subsistence, resistance, and independence is too thin to do proper justice to the Trinitarian idea of a Christian understanding of Being.

III

Foundations of a
Trinitarian Ontology

18. Starting Out from Love, with Self-Giving

For an ontology which starts from what is distinctively Christian, the basic question cannot any longer be "what endures, and what changes?" As little as this question can be permitted to drop away, it can just as little be the unquestioned starting-point. For whoever thinks starting out only from what remains, begins his thinking from a lonely starting-point, from enduring to the last, from self-intentionality. The revolutionizing force of the unadorned expression that *love alone remains* can hardly be overestimated. For if love is what remains, then what becomes central is the displacement of the center of gravity from the self to the other, movement (no longer understood in an Aristotelian fashion) and *relatio* (likewise no longer understood as a category or even as the accident weakest in Being). But relationship and movement are not instituted as some new principle from which everything would once again be inferred in a lonely deduction. Only one thing remains: active participation in that movement which *agape* itself is. This movement is the rhythm of Being; it is the rhythm of giving that gives itself.

35

19. Phenomenology of Love as Phenomenology of Being

Whence else than from a phenomenology of self-giving, from a phenomenology of love, could this new ontology be developed? Such a phenomenology of love does indeed form the background to the following propositions. It is not, however, a matter of incorporating love and self-giving into an overarching phenomenality of that which is, but, on the contrary, of reading the phenomenality of all that is, in a new and unforeshortened way, from the standpoint of love and self-giving.

This has a paradoxical consequence. It is not immediately love which we express in language, but what we have gathered from love, in the most general and formal outline. This, perhaps, expresses best of all how a phenomenology of love articulates the original self-showing of Being and beings.

20. The New Substantive: The Verb

An approach from the standpoint of love, from that of self-giving, is one which starts out with what happens, with putting love into practice [*beim Geschehen, beim Vollzug*]. In the beginning we no longer find the problem of how the subject manages to go beyond itself and come back to itself, or, to put this in another way, the problem of how substance arrives at its various differentiations, definitions, and effects, without diminishing its own inherent dignity and situation. Thinking does not go back behind the process in order to reconstruct it from an isolated point of origin. Instead, thinking is found always already or first of all in the process itself.

The substantive term [*Hauptwort*] in such a thinking is no longer the noun, but the verb. When we go along with the process [*beim Mitgang mit der Vorgang*] it is revealed what is going on, who is going on, and whence and whither the process is going.

In order to illustrate this, let us take a word which, in German, is at once a verb and a noun: *Leben* ["life, to live"]. The "thing" which the noun means is a process, a happening, life understood as a verb. The process has its identity in this going-on itself, in the manner in which it goes. To live means to go out [*Ausgehen*] from one's self. In going out, the reproduction and restitution of life takes place continually; to live means to live on. In going out, there takes place at the same time an assimilation of what is outside, an acceptance of what is outside into the inside.

This inside, however, is present only as the Whither of acceptance and the Whence of going out. The counterpoint of a living creature against other living creatures and against other beings takes place in the relationship which life itself is. Life ends, and the living creature ends, when this relationship ends.

Certainly, the connection which life is reaches still further than this; it is a connection between life and life. The inner dimension of the individual life, to which going out, communication, assimilation, and reproduction already belong, has, inseparably, an external dimension, that of living with others, in which living lives for and from the life of another.

The relationships which we see in the phenomenon of life apply, in an individual way, not only to all processes, but also to all "things." A thing, a subject, or a being can only be understood, and can only be fulfilled, in its action. And this action is a constitution, a communication, a delimitation, and an adaptation to an overarching context. Nothing "is" outside of its action—for which reason action does not mean the levelling out of a position in itself, but the very constitution of that position.

21. Unity in Plural Origination

A process is not an undivided flow—in such an undivided flow nothing at all would process. Rather a process is a relationship which happens, and which would not take place without the mutual movement towards each other, in each other, and out of each other of the poles between which this relationship is in play.

Poles, points of connection, therefore, belong here too; and the process in which they are bound up and distinguished does not level out the differences between them. But the poles do not possess any isolated position, outside what takes place; rather they are *in* what takes place. More than this, they *are* what takes place. They are this: they communicate themselves, relate themselves, give themselves over to the process and receive from the process, let it be and are let be by it.

The whole process is in each pole; the whole process is the Being of each of the poles. The poles are distinguished by the manner in which the whole process proceeds from them and by the manner in which they proceed from the process. This distinction amongst the poles in the process, however, is the distinction of the process itself; this means its articulation, from which the process acquires its unity and its divisibility, its structure.

If the new ontology's substantive [*Hauptwort*] is the verb, then the single subject is displaced by a plural origin. A process takes place in the counteracting processes in which the poles of the one process are related to each other. The one course of events has its unity, its one trajectory, and its one direction from the many poles, which, simultaneously, each from a different direction, allow each other, one upon another, to proceed to the whole process.

An example: the word. I speak the word, it goes out from me; I immediately open myself up in and to it. We can say, at least from one point of view, that nothing else gets between me and the word which I utter. I answer for it, I form it and direct it to its addressees. In this way the whole process of speaking, together with the dimensions of the word already alluded to (expression, form, addressees) are rooted in me. And yet I, too, as a speaker, together with the word which I utter, am rooted in other origins.

Language is the origin of my word. When I speak from out of myself, I lay claim to a form of language which has been shaped or at least prepared in advance by the fact that generations have already spoken before me, that human beings are created as expressive and linguistic beings, that human beings always already stand in a stream of communications. In my speech, language goes on speaking. My specific intonational nuances, my personal "grammar" are, conversely, at the least a grain of sand on the mountain range of language, a range which is permanently growing, permanently shifting. And however originally I might speak, to whatever extent I, so to speak, beget new language, my speaking is a continuing to speak, is only a grain of sand on the mountain range of spoken language.

Furthermore: you, to whom I speak, you, the addressee, are the origin of my word. My ability to speak depends on your hearing and understanding; my continuing to speak depends upon your answer; and even my beginning to speak is always already a continuing to speak on account of the beginning which you are for me, which encountering you is for me.

My word has, at least, the three origins "I," "language," "you." And it could be shown without difficulty that all three origins spring up *mutually*, each in a distinct manner, in my word; in each origin there is the whole of the same process, yet in a different way in each case. The respective contributions of the three origins cannot be quantified, but they can be distinguished from each other, through the ways in which the whole arises from each origin.

What we have gathered in relation to the example of

the "word," we could also gather from each process—even from such an apparently unambiguous process as the passage of time. Only if we understand the whole of time in and from the past, the future, and the present, can we understand time at all.

22. Play-Structure: Identity as Intensification

To read the substantive from the standpoint of the verb, things from that of processes, processes from that of their plural origin, all this does justice to the phenomenon itself. Yet it is a transformation and an intensification of usual ways of speaking and seeing.

This is particularly conspicuous in the change of the meaning of the word "identity." Identity, in our context, is experienced as an intensification, as a dramatic transformation. Life is identical with itself, in so far as it goes on, in so far as it grows; life remains life in so far as it becomes more life. Language remains language in so far as it goes on speaking, in so far as it always says more, always expresses more, always speaks more to the others. Time remains time in so far as it presses on to more, and to a larger, future.

Another example [*Beispiel*], or, rather, more than an example, is play [*Spiel*]. Whether I am playing with someone else, or, in the limit case, am only playing something by myself, there is always a reciprocal counterpoint. *I*, indeed, am playing; but the way in which my playing turns out surprises me, and places me in a new situation, to which I react. I experience myself anew in playing, and what is played is made new in playing it—this, for example, is the tension in all artistic interpretation. I am only playing Mozart well if Mozart is still Mozart. But when I play really well, Mozart becomes more Mozart-like, and I become more myself.

In essence, all processes, all domains, all relationships, can be read comprehensively when they are read from the point of view of their structure as play. In that structure, unity becomes plural origination, process becomes simultaneous progress, regress, and connection, identity becomes interpretable as intensification. The structure of play is the structure of process.

And, actually, it is play and processes that once more interest human beings, at the end of the modern age, and at the end of objective metaphysics and the metaphysics of spirit: life, for example, freedom, meaning. Such "games," such processes, are about me—but not about me alone; are about the whole—but not about a whole from which I can abstract myself; are about society—but about a society which may not once more become a Subject devouring the individual. This is the way in which all those processes, those games, are ordered, on the basis of which a new ontology discloses what is and what takes place.

23. The Restitution of the Substantive from the Verb

Everything is understood as process, as play and as reciprocal play. Must not an objection arise here: that the rights of the substantive, the ineliminable resistance of things, the seriousness of the identity which is taken on just by something's being itself, that this is given short shrift here, that distinctions founder in the merely playful, that consistency is dissolved into something vague?

This objection would be correct if headings such as process, plural origination, play, and "identity as intensification" were taken as the principles of a deduction or as the building-blocks of a system—and they would be so taken if thinking were to remain at a distance, as mere observation, if the part which thinking plays in bringing about completion were to be forgotten in the play of concepts, instead of giving itself over into what takes place in self-giving. Only in the seriousness of such a commitment does actuality actually come into play; only in such a seriousness can phenomenology escape narcissism.

Self-giving is not, however, an external addition to the phenomena already examined. Without commitment there is no play, without communicating oneself there is no speaking, without passing away there is no going on. Just such an intensification of fulfilment, however, an intensification which places all that endures continually at its disposal, brings what endures, brings the substantive back into play—in a new sense, certainly.

Giving does not hold on [*hält nicht fest*] to what it has but comprises [*enthält*] what it gives. So outside and inside are incorporated into every process; outside and inside cannot remain mixed up with each other.

43

Certainly, there is no position other than in a process, no resting-place other than in going further, no fixed point other than in a relation beyond it. But it is in just this way that permanence, that something's being itself, being distinct, is constituted. And only in this way does the process acquire its wholeness, its inner balance. Permanence, self-subsistence, and distinctness are not, however, endpoints, endpoints in which what happens would somehow run out. They are, instead, limits, at which what happens flows back into itself; they are a "skin" enclosing the tense unity of something which happens. In this limit the power of the origin is preserved: the origin can touch us. In this limit, the powerlessness of the origin is also revealed: it can be touched. Limit, as limit, is the center of going-beyond-itself. Every distinction [*Unterscheidung*] turns outwards to the decision-situation [*Entscheidungssituation*].

Going beyond and turning back reciprocally elicit each other. What opens up only to itself, does not come to itself; what opens up only away from itself, does not arrive at its Other, because it brings nothing to its Other, because it does not bring itself to its Other.

In this way, however, the "firm shape," with outline, limit, and permanence, receive their new meaning. They *are* givennesses, givennesses from which the origin—which, however, is simply giving—can be found; can be found, admittedly, in such a way, that it goes beyond itself in relation, into a relation which gives the origin *itself* beyond itself. Substance there comes to "transubstantiation," to "communion."

24. Analogy of Language—Analogy of Being

It is the meaning of form [*Gestalt*] to grasp and to attain to what "substantiates" itself in form, to bring the process back into itself and beyond itself, to open to the outside that which is nevertheless limited by the form. The "body" which a life fashions for itself, the figure in which a process unfolds, are the appearance in which the inside protects and conceals itself, and in which, at the same time, it opens itself up and communicates itself. They are the points at which this inside is at the same time both guarded as an untouchable mystery and also opened up, even relinquished, to what is outside it. Without the form the inside cannot collect itself; nor yet without form can the inside encounter the outside.

This applies not only to the particular body or to the particular figure which is produced by origins and processes and which immediately belongs to those origins and processes. It is also true, indeed most eminently so, of that form in which that which is is revealed *as such*: of the thought, of the word.

When something gives itself to be thought, it comes into its own brightness, that is, it comes to itself; it comes, however, at the same time, to its other—comes, precisely, to thinking. Everything which I say is specified by me in what is proper to it, by declaring it in the medium of its otherness, in language. Thinking, the word—and that thinking is to be thought from and towards the word goes without saying in an ontology of process, of relation—are the limits which confer identity on what is thought and said; they are the contour which can define what is proper to thinking and speaking only by letting that element meet the Other. Limit is what is "shared" between and "common" to the forces which collide at this limit, what is one in them and a third to them, their ownmost and what is alien to them, and only in this way does a passing-over take place, only in this way can a gift be given which keeps what it gives, and which gives what it takes.

This touches on the analogical character of all saying and thinking. When I say something, I bring it to light in what is proper to it [*in seinem Eigenen*], and make it over [*übereigne*] to another. It is what it is for an other. It is what it is in a common, universal sense. If we wish, in thought or in the word, to let it become apparent just as it is itself, then we cannot avoid forcing open its exclusivity, making it everyone's, translating it—that is, alienating it. And that is not a lamentable mishap, but the fulfilment of what is proper to it, since it would, precisely, disintegrate if it were to remain in itself, rather than giving itself.

The analogy of thinking and speaking, however, only fulfils and discloses the analogy of Being, Being which "is" just as the fulfilment of passing-over, of communion, of self-giving. *Analogia entis* means Being's reciprocal into-each-other and out-of-each-other. This for-each-other unconceals itself as the meaning of this Being.

This also affects the meaning of what we said earlier, when we were, in a formal and general way, finding the language for the structure of a new ontology. The unequivocality of definitions is the unequivocality of a line, against which several things collide, touching each other and joining each other as they are divided. The unequivocality of a form in itself corresponds to its equivocal reference beyond itself.

The same structure: a process arising from many origins, a process in contrapuntal processes, a process as the same and ever new, a process as recession into itself and as procession beyond itself—all this is not a universal law under which the most various phenomena might be subsumed; it is not a principle from which everything can be deduced; it is not a reduction under a common denominator of everything which cannot be derived from something else. Rather it is a release into the peculiar and irreplaceable, a limit or border, precisely, from which whatever currently obtains is repelled into its own distinctiveness, and by virtue of which it yet, at the same time, communicates with the other.

The new ontology does not take away from thinking the capacity to renew itself in relation to any given phenomenon or in any given process. Thinking has its own self-identical formal structures, which are valid in themselves. Yet thinking does not think these structures; rather, in these structures it thinks that which gives itself, ever new and ever different, to be thought by it. In this way, the structures themselves, too, are transformed; they become ever new.

25. Dimensions of Analogy

Thinking and language mark the limits at which things distinct from each other come up against other, are distinguished from each other, are given to each other, are inaugurated and alienated at the same time. We have understood this multiple relatedness, this combination of unification and distinguishing, as analogy. What is it that meets, at its connecting limit or border? Being and thinking border on each other; being is delimited from being, domain from domain; speaker and listener, speaker and speaker, enter into their positions and into the unity of speaking.

The play between being and being, between thinking and Being, between speaking and speaking, is always different. And yet all play is connected; all play is playing a single game.

Yet that this single game "goes on" points, for its part, to a plural origin. We play it, each from out of himself; we play it, but as played by each other, directed to play the part of a We. Yet in so far as we play it, we assent to the inalterable character of this game as a law unto itself; the game itself is the origin of our playing it. What is more, in the reciprocal relation of game and players something is initiated which goes beyond the game itself. Why is there play and not rather not-play? How does it come about that we play the game, can do nothing other than play, and yet are set free in play and free to play?

We owe our existence to the game, the game of one with another, yet we and the game both owe our existence to what is set apart from play, and which calls forth our answer and our answerability, that which, as the most hidden, gives itself to us in the manifest gift of the game, and which, for its part, alone permits us wholly to give ourselves and alone rewards us for doing so.

From below, seen from the perspective of the immediacy of the game, this may be an ultimate, the highest, the most analogical of all analogies, that in which we most experience Being and thinking as the limits which, in the game, instruct us about the game: the mystery, God Himself, shines out into the game, in the play of analogy.

26. The Question of What is New in the New Ontology

The perspective from below does not, however, bring what is new in this "new ontology" immediately or unequivocally into view. Are there not, in the tradition of Western metaphysics and in the attempts to overcome it, approaches aplenty pointing in the same direction? Thomas Aquinas's thinking about analogy and participation; the way in which Bonaventure expounds an *ars aeterna*, or the way in which Nicholas of Cusa thinks the reciprocal being-in of whole and individual; the thought-model of Descartes, who, although this is obscured by the history of his reception, illuminates the highly differentiated network of mutual revelation and conditioning by which the self, God, and world, and the paths from each to the others, are mediated; the last thoughts of German idealism, in, for example, the late philosophy of Schelling; the doctrine of the simultaneity of unification and division in Baader, his "eucharistic" understanding of world and form; the thinking of a Rosenzweig about language and relation; Heidegger's meditations on the unthinkable offering of time and Being; and, finally, the structural ontology of Heinrich Rombach—all this traces the arc of a broad convergence of these motifs and approaches, however distinct they might be from each other.

What is new in the new ontology is its approach to a depth which cannot be disclosed from below: to the threefold mystery of God, which is revealed to us in faith. The mystery of this mystery is love, self-giving. From out of love, all Being, all thinking, everything that happens is disclosed in its own structure; the *relecture* of what is revealed to faith is brought about through immediate regard to the phenomenon of love. Thinking learns how to think anew in this "phenomenology"; it is transformed by becoming a going-along with the way of self-giving, the way of love. Thinking discovers, in this, that just this originality and immediacy of thinking is its own.

27. Trinitarian Answers

"He that spared not his own Son, but delivered him up for us all, how shall he not with him also freely give us all things?" (Romans 8:32). This primordial experience of faith is grounded in Jesus's death and resurrection.

We come to know that Jesus has given Himself for us, but that His gift of Himself is *God's* gift, and that in this gift everything is transformed—life and the world, the meaning of Being, everything whatever—because the gift is given from His origin, from the rhythm of *His* self-giving. This is the inner justification, and, indeed, the necessity, of a Trinitarian ontology.

It is disclosed only to whoever can give himself to this divine self-giving, to whoever can incorporate not only his thinking, but his very existence—and this not only privately, but in all his relationships—into the answering movement of self-giving: "all are yours; and ye are Christ's; and Christ is God's" (1 Cor 3:23–24). Yet whoever, from the indemonstrable and ineliminable decision of faith to love, draws the conclusion of loving self-sacrifice, discovers in the things, in the relationships, in the domains and events of this world, what they most deeply say and show *of themselves*. He breaks through into a new middle of phenomenality, which also bears witness of itself to the one who stands outside it—not automatically, certainly, and not compulsorily, but as inviting him to a decision.

The proposition, correct in itself, that God's external relationships bring God into play not as threefold but as one, has, ever since Augustine, stood in the way of tracing the Trinitarian line. If, however, the one God is self-giving and if the "immanent" Trinity is, precisely, incipient in the "economic" Trinity, and if its incipience itself has an economic intention—distribution, sharing [*Teilgabe*] in God's innermost point and our being taken into the innermost of God—then the analogy of Being becomes, also, an analogy of the Trinity. Everything fulfils itself and brings that which is its ownmost to perfection by entering into its relatedness, into its being-beyond itself, into its self-having as self-giving, into its character as to and for each other. Everything has in itself the rank and value which it has in the happening of love. The old proposition, then, retains its validity: *relatio Dei ad extra est una*. But *una* means: common. God makes a present of Himself. Father and Son and Spirit are each in their own way at work in this self-giving-away, and are each in their own way detectable in it. Our answer, our thoughts and deeds, relate to the one God—but the unity of our answer is constituted precisely in entering into and repeating the moments in which is constituted the unity of the way in which the Trinity happens.

To make this the basis of our understanding of Being and of our concrete comportment—to be, that is, in earnest with such a Trinitarian ontology—this would indeed be something new. And it would be a needed turn in an age in which, as scarcely ever before, the contingency of thinking and Being, the questionability of subject and substance, the disappearance of God, the world and the human being, and threats to freedom and to meaning have become everyday experiences.

28. The Plausibility of a Trinitarian Ontology

Whoever believes in Jesus Christ believes in a love

which does not merely retrospectively make good what just is, as it is. He believes in a love which stands at the beginning, in the middle, and at the end. He believes in love as the meaning of Being. Love, however, is, when seen from a Christian point of view, in the profoundest sense, a threefold love. Seen from above, from the standpoint of revelation, a Trinitarian ontology, therefore, follows consistently. Seen from below, from immediate experience, from direct observation of that which is, this does not necessarily follow. Resistant self-assertion or dissolution into what is finally unintelligible, blind facticity or immanent lawlikeness threaten to be the final information given to beings about themselves. But anyone who failed to ask questions which go beyond this information would underestimate that to which history testifies, which is imparted in the tendency of human beings and of creation towards meaning and fulfilment, that which is at play in the unconstruable and indissoluble togetherness of Being and thinking, of I and Thou, of humanity and the world. It must at least lead us to think that, even in respect of the data of experience, a Trinitarian ontology integrates more than other ontologies.

Does not one thing, however, remain left out of a Trinitarian ontology: that which is not subsumed, guilt, loneliness, mourning over finitude, the failure to reach one's goal? If such experiences were negated or relativized into a merely contrastive transitional moment in the system, then the credibility of the whole would, at any rate, be at stake.

It is, however, seen theologically, the deepest point of a Trinitarian ontology that in the kenosis of the Son all finitudes and contradictions are taken on by the event of divine self-giving. In the cry of "why?" on the Cross and in the silence of Sheol, into which the Son descends, everything is integrated and yet nothing is appropriated. The hope which is evidenced in, for example, the letter to the Romans, is clearly enough the opposite of ideology, oppression, and self-assured exploitation.

29. Levels of Trinitarian Happening

Not only does Trinitarian ontology have to prove itself by its philosophical power of integration, but it must also, without coercion or arbitrariness, integrate the whole of revelation theologically; it must allow that revelation to become transparent in respect of its Trinitarian center.

Here it will have to suffice that we mark the levels on which such a theological integration should be carried out, and sketch the ordering of the movements from one level to another.

The entry-point is the event of the "economic" Trinity: Jesus reveals the Father; the Father apotheosizes Him as the Son; the Spirit reveals the affiliation of each to the other, the Father's and the Son's affiliations to us, and our affiliation to the divine life.

This course of events is not, however, an external "supplement" to that which God is, but is His innermost, ownmost mystery: the path leads from the "economic" to the "immanent" Trinity.

Because the immanent Trinity unfolds economically, the way in which creation flows into its inclusion in the life of the Trinity is revealed as the *oikonomia* of creation. The ordering of creation is an anticipation of its Trinitarian fulfilment and completion. This fulfilment and completion is an extra gift added to the gift of creation; but the positive meaning of the first gift only becomes visible in the second.

The faithful, the community of the church: this is the point at which creation enters the Trinitarian happening of being-given and giving. Being-in-Christ is the new mode of existence into which the believer incorporates himself and his world. Jesus's relation to the Father, the Trinitarian ethos, becomes the ethos of self-fulfilment and world-fulfilment.

Being-in-Christ, moreover, does not only open into the life of the Trinity, but also opens a Trinitarian relationship *between* us, in the world. The Johannine "As" wishes to be in play between us. We are to love *one another*, as Jesus loved us; indeed, we are to be one *with* each other, as He and the Father are one (cf. John 13:35, 17:21ff.).

A Trinitarian present moment such as we are called to stands as yet, admittedly, under the law of time. It is, as present, self-giving to a future, whose gift remains, therefore, awaited. More than this, time as such is manifested as that present which, in giving itself, is to pass away into a future which is the final, perfected gift, stretching beyond time. Trinitarian ontology is, as such, eschatologically open.

IV

Appendix: Consequences
of a Trinitarian Ontology

30. Philosophical Consequences

Some philosophical problems are difficult to solve not
only by means of a deductive or constructive ontology,
but even by means of a merely inductive or descriptive
ontology. New light is shed on such problems by mea-
suring thought against the Trinitarian model, by taking
the analogy of thinking and Being seriously—an analogy which is mediated by the self-giving of the primordial mystery of the Trinity to all creation.

This thesis could be confirmed, for instance, by considering the way in which analysis and synthesis, Being
and happening, persistence and the event, freedom and
necessity each mutually include the other.

If—let us repeat it—love is what endures, if to move
away from oneself is to move towards oneself, if to relin-
quish one's essence is to inaugurate it, then the indemonstrable, apparently mutually exclusive poles belong
to each other, without being collapsed into each other.
This to and fro, of course, becomes evident, admittedly,
only in its fulfilment, only in verbal relatedness, and not
in substantivistic isolation.

Let us take up, at least in outline, the headings mentioned. Analytic propositions are essentially tautologies. The predicate gives no new information with respect to the subject. That analytic propositions are possible—in the end, that thinking is thinking and Being Being—can surprise or even astonish thinking. One might say—that's just how it is; it's an irrefutable given. But whence is such givenness given? In analysis, therefore, a primordial, giving synthesis announces itself.

Is it, then, correct to trace all the necessities of thinking and being back to an act which would govern them, an act of divine caprice? Just the opposite. Thinking is to just the same extent placed in aporias, whether God's freedom is ranked *beneath* the necessities of Being and thinking, or whether that freedom, as arbitrary government, is ranked *above* those necessities. If, however, self-giving is the pure beginning, these false alternatives are resolved. Self-giving is departure, is being-away from oneself. This is just what gives self-giving its identity, this is what it persists in. It preserves itself by giving itself away. The new element (freedom, synthesis) is the self-same (necessity, analysis). The phenomenological concept of identity as intensification is made good. Only in self-sameness can newness prove itself; self-sameness, however, originates in the event, in the newness of self-giving.

The young Schelling had the brilliant idea of considering the unity of freedom and necessity through the phenomenon of art. The work of art is a work of art by virtue of its inner attunement, by virtue of its necessity. This necessity is the necessity of free artistic production crystallizing as form. This freedom is the freedom to bring about a convincing and necessary form. Cannot the way in which freedom and necessity mutually include each other be, however, more radically inferred, inferred from the origin, in the phenomenality of self-giving?

It goes without saying that what results from the mutual inclusion of freedom and necessity is not some sort of "freedom" on God's part to circumvent the law of identity, nor that God would lie under some sort of "necessity" of letting the non-divine, letting creation be. The freedom of self-giving is an intratrinitarianly pure, necessary unity in itself, and is, at the same time, freedom to go beyond itself, freedom to let what is non-necessary be—that is, to let it not be necessary.

Self-giving as the pure beginning, as the unconditioned event: this approach to thinking displays its highest result, or its first origin, in the basic theological declarations about the Trinitarian God. Nowhere is the radicality of the beyond-itself, and, just by virtue of that, of Being-in-itself as conspicuous as in the doctrine of the intratrinitarian processions. Let us recall, here, Bonaventure's idea of God as the highest goodness, whose pure remaining-in-Himself is also pure self-outpouring.

The perspective from this center of unconditional self-giving confirms and clarifies the mutual inclusion of analysis and synthesis, Being and happening, persistence and the event, freedom and necessity.

31. Theological Consequences

These philosophical consequences point towards the theological ones, which, in turn, provide the key to moving forward to a new philosophical understanding.

The immutability of God and the history of God—the dialectic between infinite and finite freedom—the correspondence between eternal begetting and incarnation, and, at the same time, the reciprocal passage in and out of each other of the divine and the human in the hypostatic union, become legible in the counterpoint of self-giving, in the analogy which springs up out of self-giving itself.

Here we must restrict ourselves to even more abbreviated indications. If all analysis is grounded in the primordial synthesis of self-giving; if all necessity is an interpretation of the freedom which sets it in motion and which bears it up; then in divine Trinitarian being-itself, the Other, the creature, is as un-necessary as possible, and creation is then just as much something which is always already overtaken by divine being-itself as it is something new which goes beyond divine being-itself. This apparent dialectic is only an interpretation of self-giving itself as what grounds the *analogia entis*.

These relationships find their sharpest point where God not only gives permission to his Other to be itself, but where He also gives Himself over into his Other, in the incarnation and in what follows from it, from Holy Saturday to Easter and Pentecost.

Where God gives Himself over wholly into his Other, it follows that He is giving Himself over, precisely, into finite freedom. It can be said that monothelitism is the most sublime misrecognition of the fact that the incarnation is in earnest. If the meaning of the incarnation is God's having given Himself to the utmost degree, then Jesus's human freedom is the most exposed finite freedom that there is, that is to say, that freedom whose free obedience, whose free self-giving to the Father, signifies the most *incomprehensible* self-giving. But just at this point it is no contradiction that *this* self-giving stands within the never-failing simplicity of divine freedom, of divine self-giving. The highest drama and the purest ease coincide.

And, beyond this, it becomes clear that God's revelation reaches its uttermost point in the *communicatio idiomatum*, which, without this context, often appears strangely artificial. The human element in the human being Jesus becomes the most direct proclamation of God, for God is most Himself where He is most self-giving and self-relinquishing.

32. Consequences For How We Think, Speak, and Exist

Trinitarian ontology is not only something thought contains, but something thought carries out. To think Trinitarian ontology means with one's thinking and speaking—but also, therefore, with one's very existence—to enter into its rhythm oneself.

I can see only whatever I permit to be given to me; I can see only that to which I give myself. Seeing itself happens only in the simultaneity of a giving projection [*Entwurf*] and a receptive understanding—a simultaneity which is no compromise, but is the novelty and unity of seeing. Spiritual performance, therefore, stands on the three lines of the away-from-me, the towards-me, and the including and distinguishing mutual relation of these two. The dynamics of thinking and Being are always to accept, always to begin, always to connect.

These three positions, disclosed in the way the Trinity happens, are the constituents of any individual performance. Not only of my performance, but of the performance which, as thinking, speaking, and Being, goes beyond the 'I': the performance of the We, the performance of the between.

Any individual performance must indeed unite in itself all the moments mentioned, yet in the common performance of partners different roles emerge: speaking initiative, listening answer, and mediating inspiration are different ways of being at the same time the whole of the conversation.

Here there emerges an alternative to those conceptions of society which see in it only a sum total of isolated individuals, or a collective subject, or the product of a merely functional series of bonds. A new ontology impels us towards a new society. Such a society differs from a totalitarian society, however conceived, in which the mutual relations of all individuals are alienated so as to become mere instruments of an ideology, even the ideology of a total society. It is no less distinct, however, from a society which, supposedly on the basis of free-

dom, does not lead beyond the synchronization of ego-
isms and solitudes; in such a society the relation
between individuals threatens to become a mere along-
side-each-other or past-each-other, in a mere objectivity and functionality—by which, however, freedom,
which lives only in relation, would itself be hollowed
out. Only the "Trinitarian model" makes it possible to
understand every individual as, in his own fashion, the
origin of society, and, at the same time, to understand
society as more than the sum of individuals; to see that
society has a single, common life and that this is nevertheless the life of each individual. I, the other, and the
whole become the point of departure, the goal and the
middle of a movement.

To see and form everything in the image of the Trinity—this could be understood as arbitrary whimsy or as
fanatical arrogance; it could appear to be divine play or
playing with the divine, where the latter should not be
mixed with the human. If, however, we take seriously
the new perspective afforded by analogy, if we understand it as a making-strange which is the cost of making something our own, then the "game" retains both
its limits and its seriousness.

33. The Unity of Theory, Spirituality, and Community

Trinitarian ontology in and as performance could show
us a way of getting beyond the separation which we
necessarily experience between theory, personal praxis,

and the shapes of communities and societies. The theory of a Trinitarian ontology has, as congruent with it, as its condition and as its consequence, a corresponding spirituality. But it is not only I, the individual, who am moulded and challenged by this; I am at the same time pointed out towards a new relationship to the Thou, to the We, to society in all its domains. In the context of a Trinitarian ontology, there might grow something like what was intimated by the synthesis of the great spiritual vocations in the church: they combined in one their theology and philosophy, their manners of praying and of living, and their power to work on and shape society.

Such a synthesis would be a timely and distinctively Christian answer to the errors and disappointments produced by the social and ecclesiastical climate at the end of the modern age. Although merely postulating this does not do what is needed, it can help to make us clear-sighted and prepared for the first signs.

There are hints of the contours of the spirituality, the theory, and the community which would correspond to a Trinitarian ontology.

To begin with *spirituality*, with the sustaining "brief formula" of faith, from which we can surmise the whole plenitude of what is to be believed: it is "we have known and believed the love that God hath shown to us" (1 John 4:16). The love which God Himself is, which gives itself in Jesus, and which gives us the Spirit, so that we may give ourselves to ourselves, is the foundation.

Such a spirituality is *contemplative*, since it attends to the traces of this love in everything, finds love in everything and especially in what is darkest and strangest: in the Cross. That is where love has most revealed itself, has most given itself. Self-giving is not only the ground, but also the measure. Contemplation is not an observation which merely registers what it sees, but absorption. What gives itself to be seen is love, and that which is capable of seeing is, once again, love alone, which gives itself. And love gives itself precisely in the most unalloyed way, gives itself without reservation, with Mary, at the foot of the Cross.

Such spirituality is in its contemplation at the same time *active, secular.* It is service. It is attuned to God's self-giving, which goes to the edge, to the uttermost. Not only does the answer to God's love happen on the Cross; what also takes place there is community with God's love for the world. "Having loved his own which were in the world, he loved them unto the end" (John 13:1). It is for us to love as He loved us (cf. John 15:12).

Such a spirituality is, in its contemplation and action, *communitarian.* Self-giving is not only its vertical direction, above and below. Self-giving is also its horizontal direction. It is amongst us, in our community, that the life of God is to be lived, that it is to become a world, to become a space in which the Lord dwells so that the world may believe (cf. John 17:21 ff., Matthew 18:20).

To spirituality correspond *theory* and *theology*.

Theology is *traditionary*. For if God has given Himself, theology cannot permit anything of the *traditio* of this self-giving to fall to the ground. In all things theology must give thanks for and disclose the one thing, God's self-giving.

Such a theology is at the same time *current* theology, *everyday* theology. It must look, with God, whither God's love looks, whither He gives Himself and wishes to give Himself: towards these human beings and this world.

Such a theology is, once again, *communitarian, ecclesial.* It does not depend upon sudden flashes of individual inspiration, but upon individual self-giving and receiving; it depends upon living with each other and seeing each other. It is not ecclesial only in its care not to contradict the doctrine of the church; it is actively ecclesial as an expression and revelation of lived unity.

Community itself—in the church, but also in society—falls under the same law.

Its life does not consist in its members doing as they like or arranging things as they like. It has standards, it has authority, it has *obligations.* The Christian knows and experiences the fact that the measure of all community is the love of the one who has given Himself to the uttermost and whose love is the most extreme demand.

Such a community is not a community of entitlements or of consumption, but a community of *service.* The highest dignity, the highest right, the greatest initiative of an individual, his unjustifiable claim, is to take first place in loving, to take first place in serving.

Such a community is not an association formed to

pursue a particular goal, but is *life itself.* For if this life takes place according to the measure of Trinitarian self-giving, then all loss becomes gain, all losing of self becomes a finding of self—only, of course, in and through the Cross. The individual and the whole stop competing with each other, and become, in their recip-rocal relationship, the space in which the divine life bears witness to itself and can truly, in a worldly and preliminary way, be experienced.